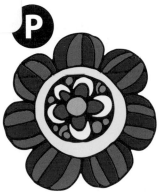

Primary colors: These are the colors that cannot be obtained by mixing any other colors; they are yellow, blue, and red.

Secondary colors: These colors are obtained by mixing two primary colors in equal parts; they are green, purple, and orange.

Tertiary colors: These colors are obtained by mixing one primary color and one secondary color.

Coloring Ideas

Color each section of the drawing (every general area, not every tiny shape) in one single color. This will take less time and can change the overall look of the drawing.

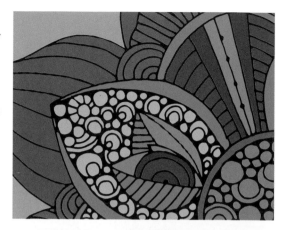

Within each section, color each detail (small shape) in alternating colors. This creates a nice varied and symmetrical effect.

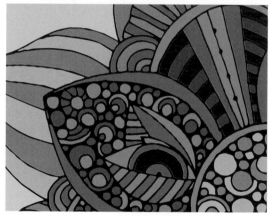

Leave some areas white to add a sense of space and lightness to the illustration. Just because it's there doesn't mean it has to be colored!

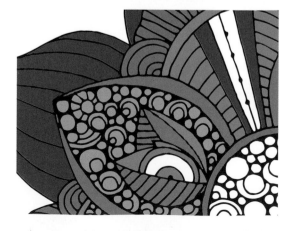

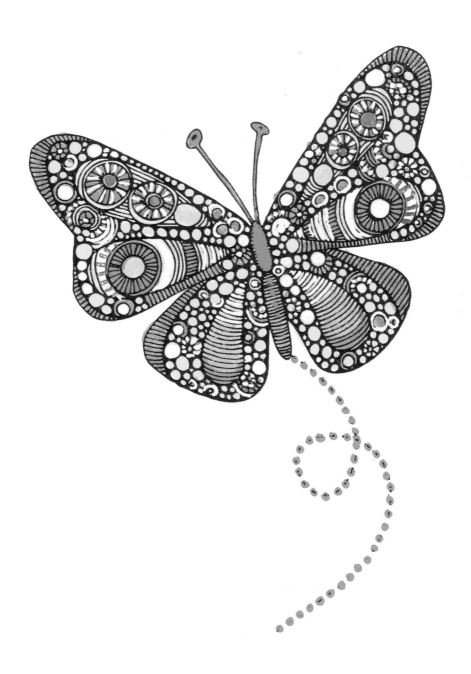

Dual Brush Markers (Tombow), Gel Pens (Sakura).
Bright Tones. Color by Marie Browning.

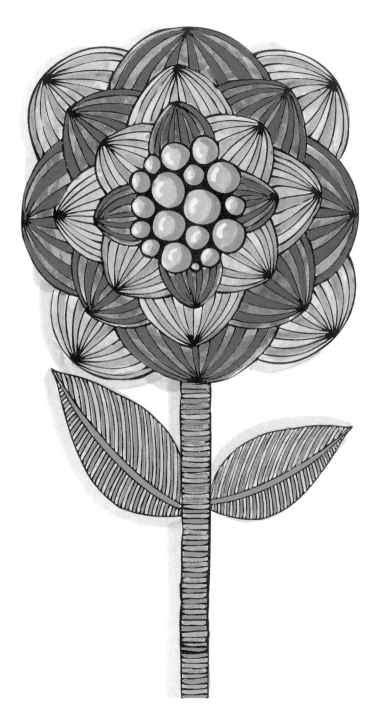

Dual Brush Markers (Tombow), Gel Pens (Sakura).
Analogous Tones. Color by Marie Browning

Coloring Tools

Using whatever medium you like, you can take these delightful drawings into a new world of color. Different coloring tools can really lend different effects and moods to an illustration— for example, markers make a vibrant statement while colored pencils offer a softer feel. Have fun experimenting with some of these mediums:

- Markers
- Colored pencils
- Colored pens
- Gel pens
- Watercolors
- Crayons

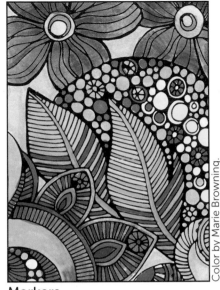

Color by Marie Browning.

Markers
Dual Brush Markers (Tombow).
Bright Tones.

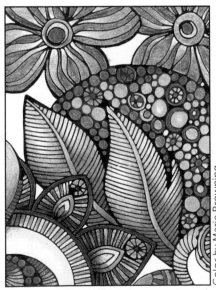

Color by Marie Browning.

Colored Pencils
Irojiten Colored Pencils (Tombow).
Vivid Tones.

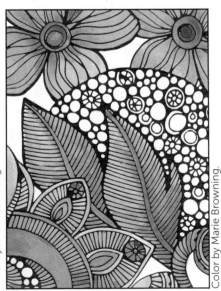

Color by Marie Browning.

Watercolors
Watercolors (Winsor & Newton).
Analogous Tones.

Color Theory

With color, illustrations take on a life of their own. Remember: when it comes to painting and coloring, there are no rules. The most fun part is to play with color, relax, and enjoy the process and the beautiful finished result. Feel free to mix and match colors and tones. Work your way from primary colors to secondary colors to tertiary colors, combining different tones to create all kinds of different effects. If you aren't familiar with color theory, here is a quick, easy guide to the basic colors and combinations you will be able to create.

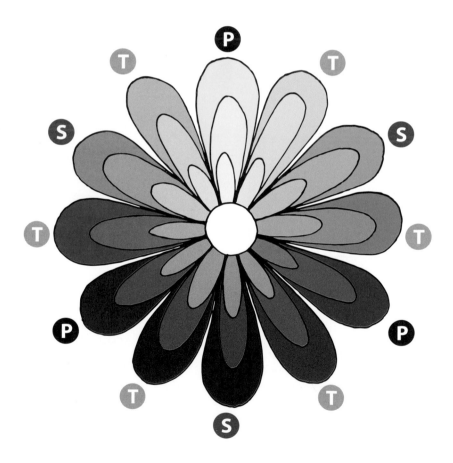

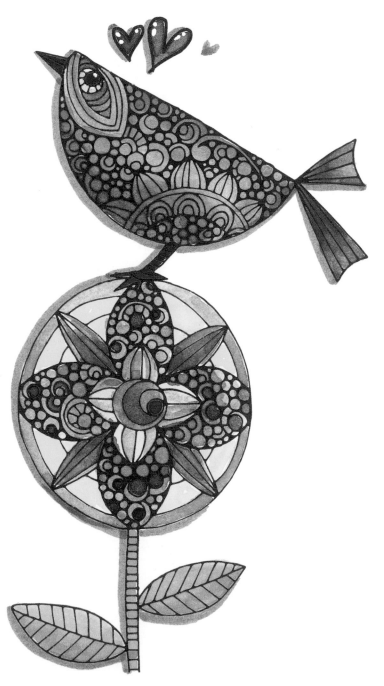

Watercolors (Winsor & Newton). Bright Tones.
Color by Marie Browning.

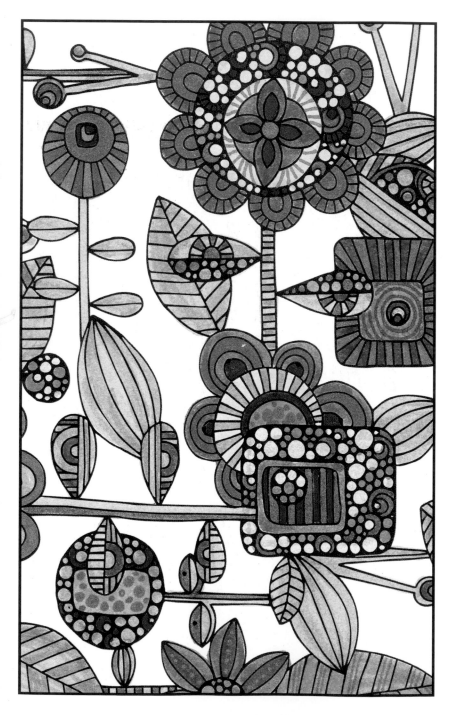

Dual Brush Markers (Tombow), Metallic Gel Pens (Sakura). Jewel Tones. Color by Marie Browning.

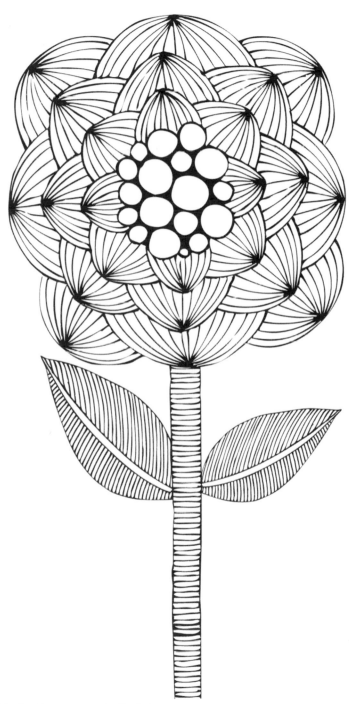

Flowers leave some of their fragrance
in the hand that bestows them.

—Chinese proverb

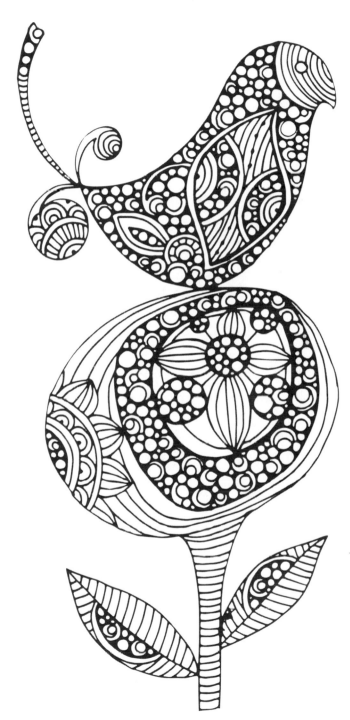

Remember that your natural state is joy.

—**Wayne Dyer**

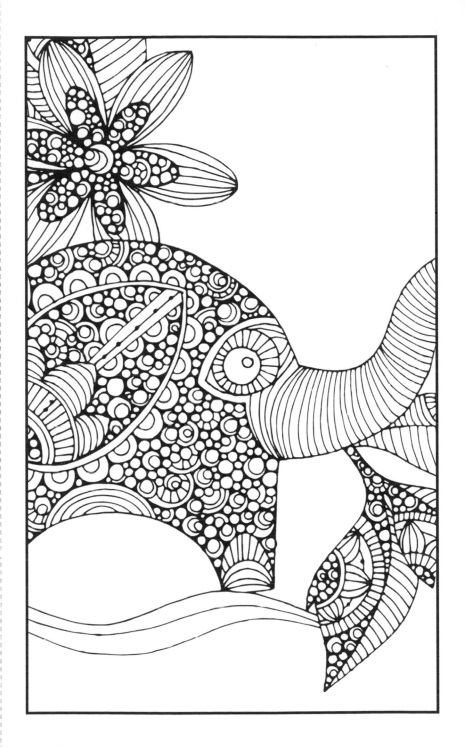

I've decided to be happy, because
it is good for my health.

—Voltaire

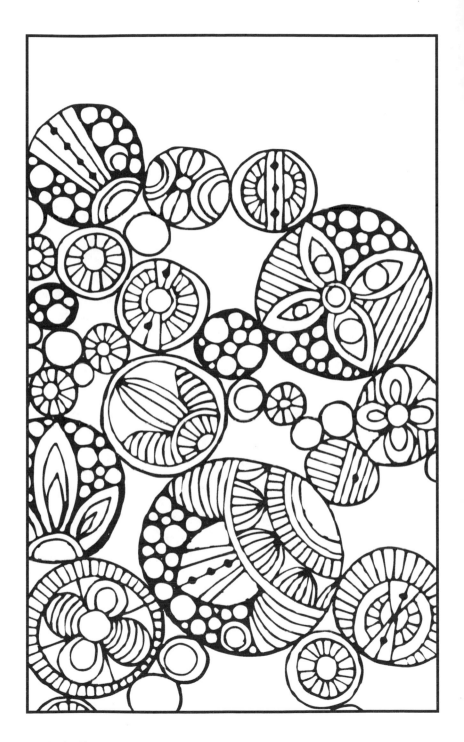

Turn your face to the sun and the shadows will fall behind you.

—Maori proverb

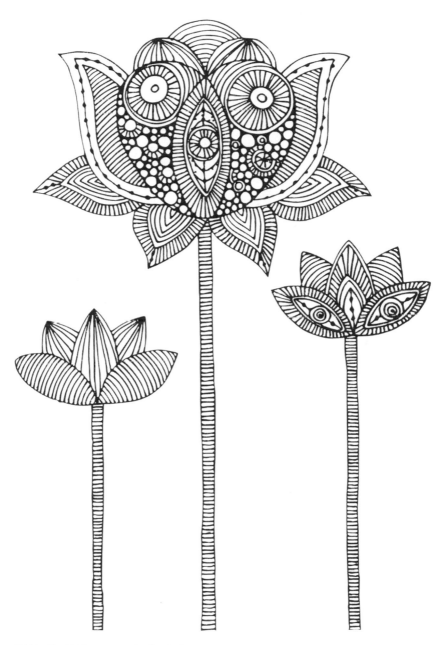

Be happy for this moment.
This moment is your life.

—Omar Khayyam

_____
_____
_____
_____
_____
_____
_____
_____
_____
_____

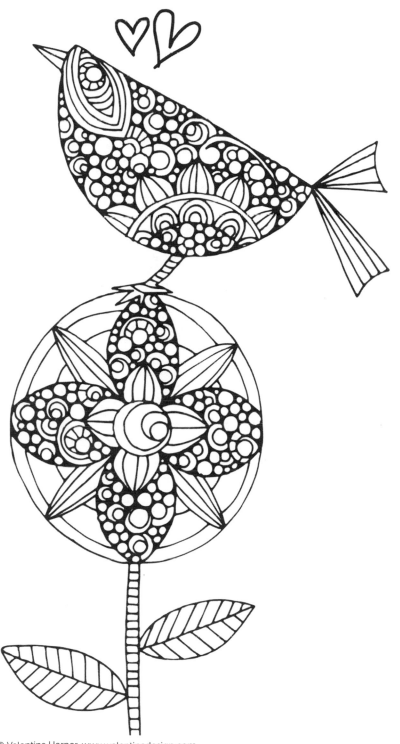

Dream higher than the sky and
deeper than the ocean.

—Unknown

_____

_____

_____

_____

_____

_____

_____

_____

_____

_____

_____

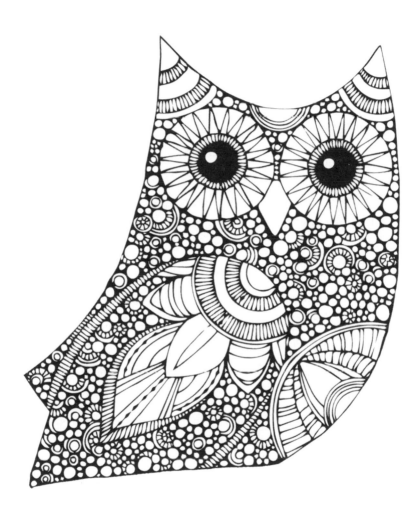

Knowledge is knowing what to say.
Wisdom is knowing when to say it.

—Unknown

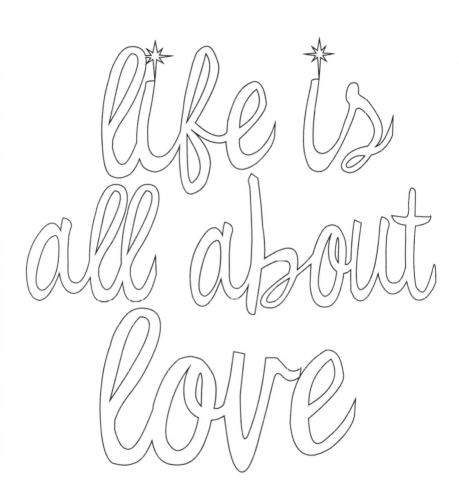

When you love and laugh abundantly
you live a beautiful life.

—Unknown

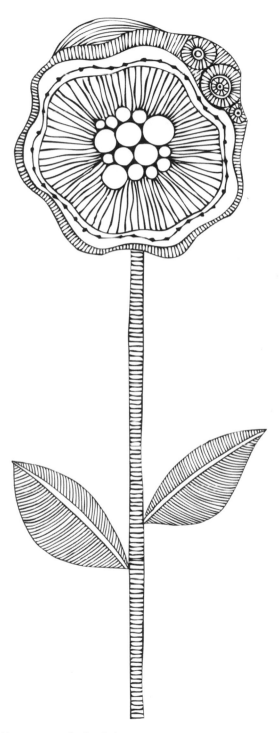

With freedom, books,
flowers, and the moon,
who could not be happy?

—Oscar Wilde

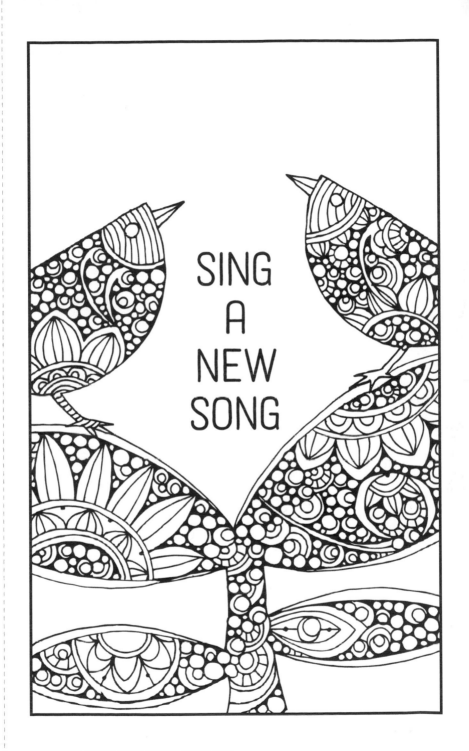

Nothing in life is to be feared.
It is only to be understood.

—Marie Curie

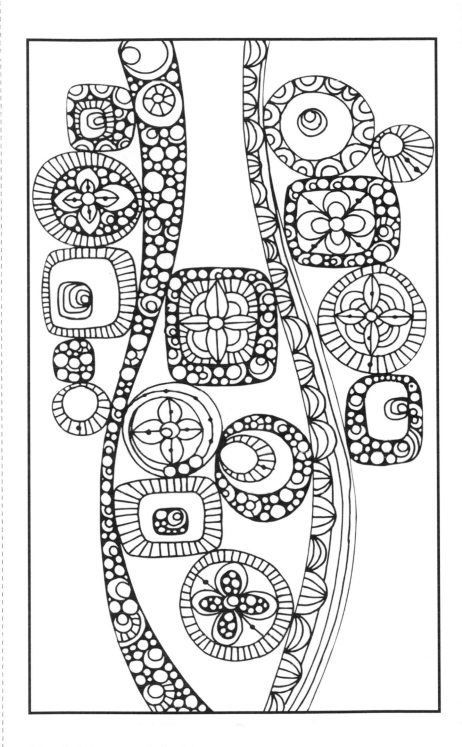

The world needs dreamers
and the world needs doers.
But above all, the world needs
dreamers who do.

—Sarah Ban Breathnach

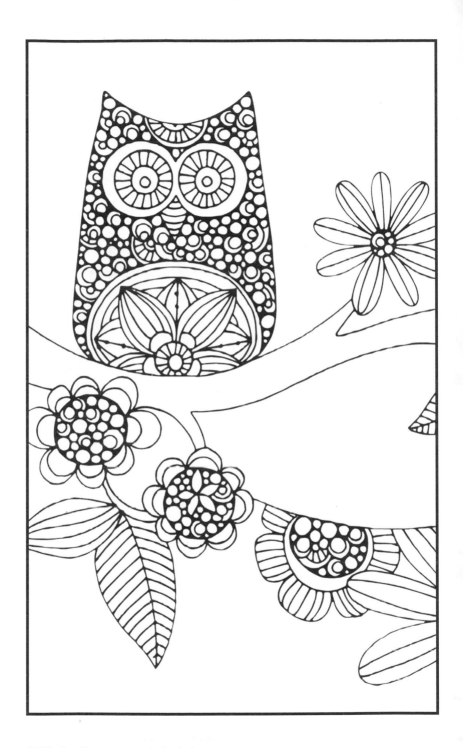

Be who you are and say what you feel because those who mind don't matter and those who matter don't mind.

—Dr. Seuss

_____

_____

_____

_____

_____

_____

_____

_____

_____

_____

life is beautiful

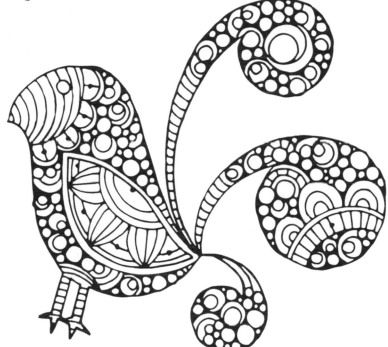

You can't do anything about
the length of your life,
but you can do something
about its width and depth.

—Evan Esar

_____
_____
_____
_____
_____
_____
_____
_____
_____
_____

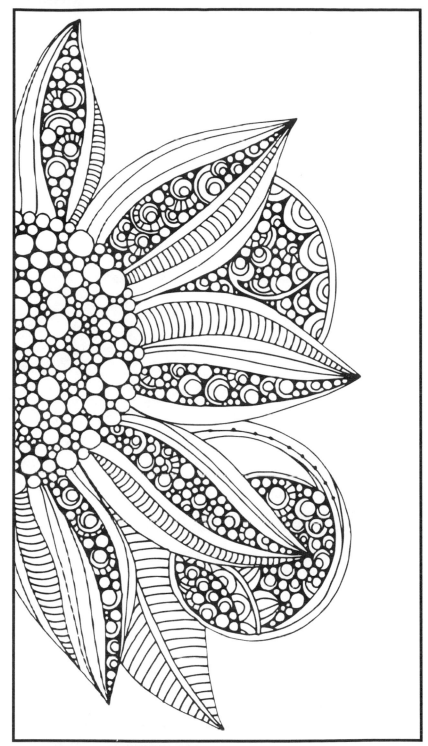

Take pride in how far you have come and have faith in how far you can go.

—Unknown

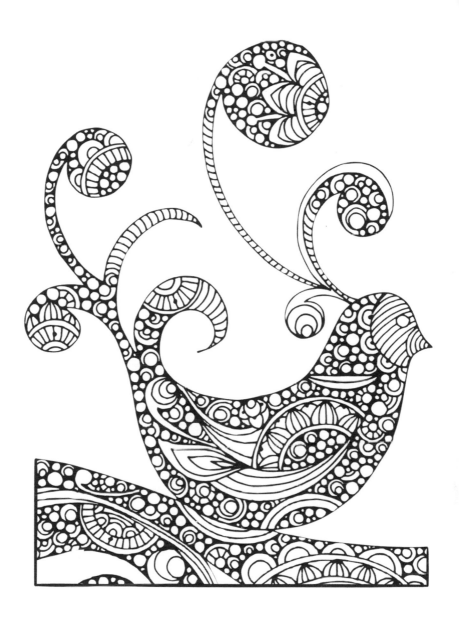

You can, you should, and if you're brave enough to start, you will.

—Stephen King

_____
_____
_____
_____
_____
_____
_____
_____
_____
_____

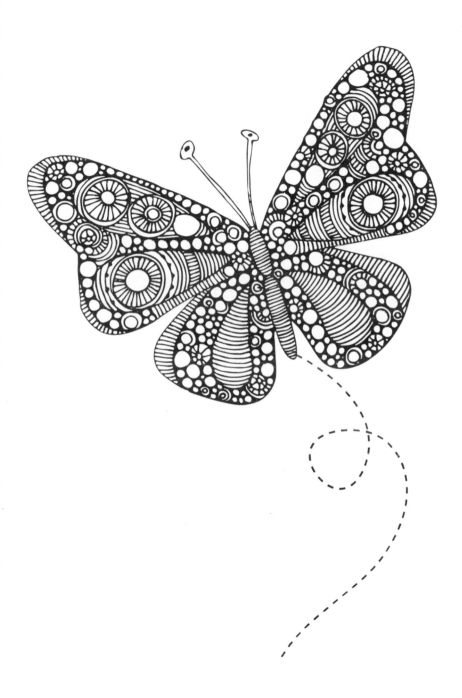

No pessimist ever discovered
the secrets of the stars,
or sailed to an uncharted land,
or opened a new heaven
to the horizon of the spirit.

—Helen Keller

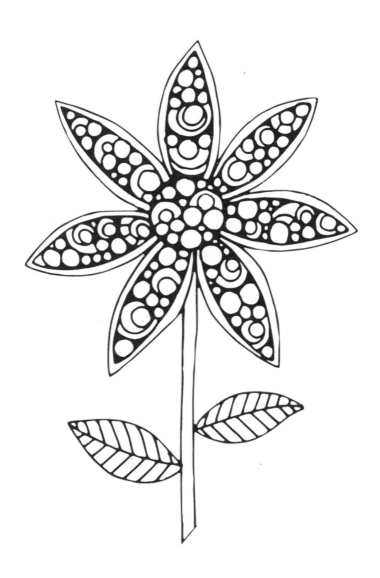

Friends are flowers in the garden of life.

—Proverb

_____
_____
_____
_____
_____
_____
_____
_____
_____
_____

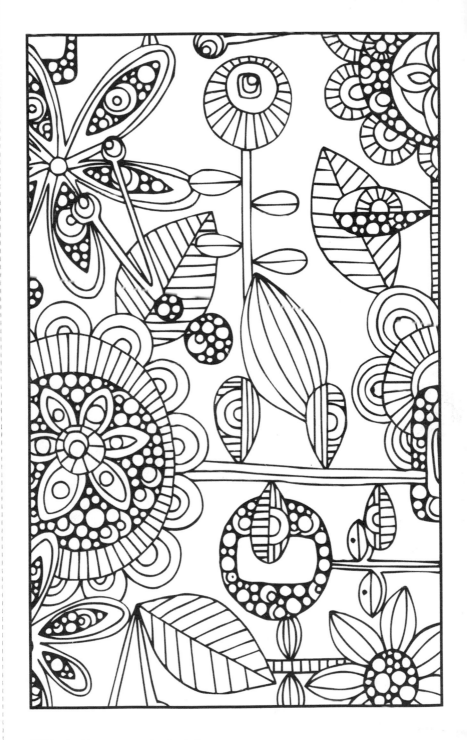

A weed is but an unloved flower.

—Ella Wheeler Wilcox

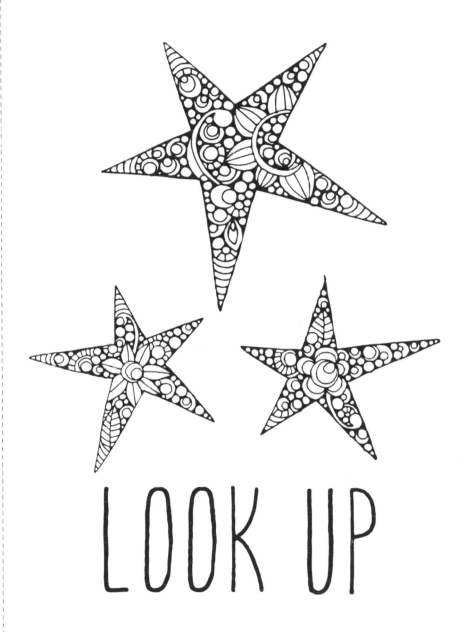

LOOK UP

Only in the darkness can you see the stars.

—Martin Luther King, Jr.

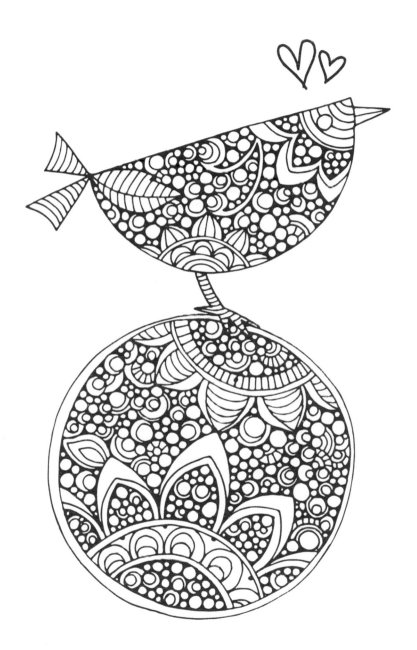

Hope appears on the horizon each morning
in the form of a brand new day.

—Unknown

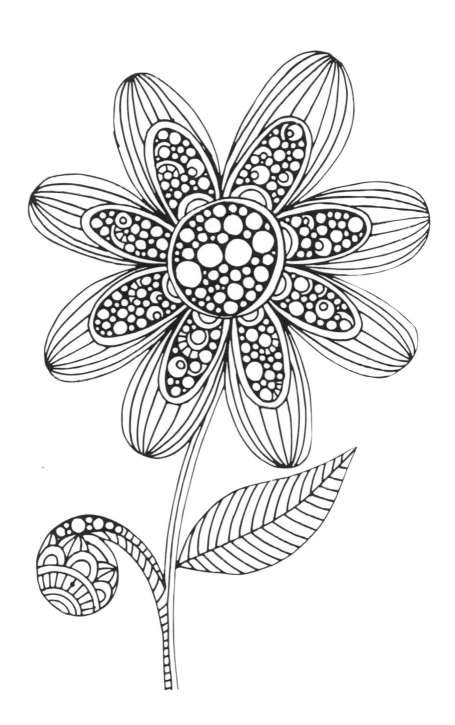

Everything grows better with love.

—Unknown

_____

_____

_____

_____

_____

_____

_____

_____

_____

_____

LET LOVE GROW

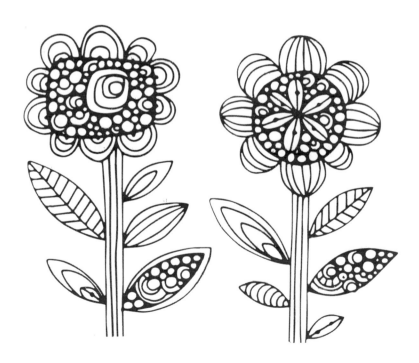

Love is old,
love is new,
love is all,
love is you.

—The Beatles

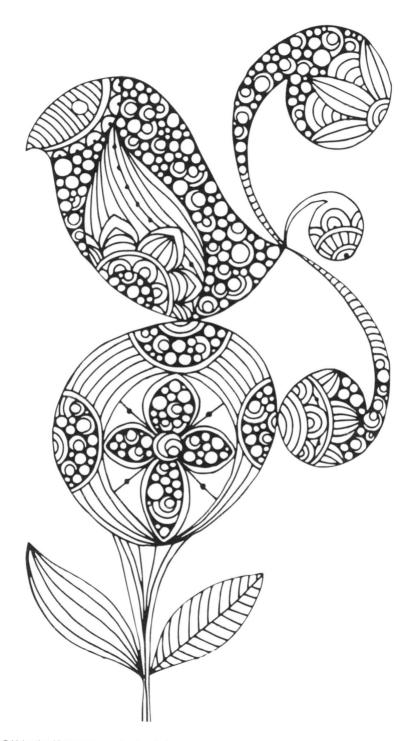

Whether you think you can or
think you can't—you are right.

—Henry Ford

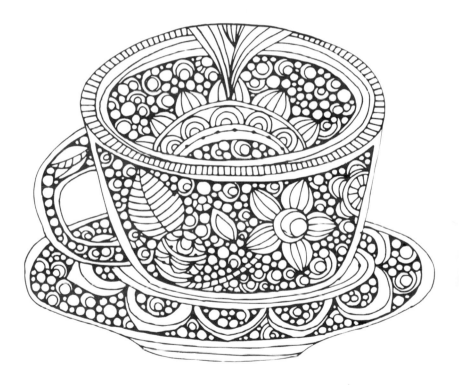

Three grand essentials to happiness
in this life are something to do,
something to love, and something
to hope for.

—Joseph Addison

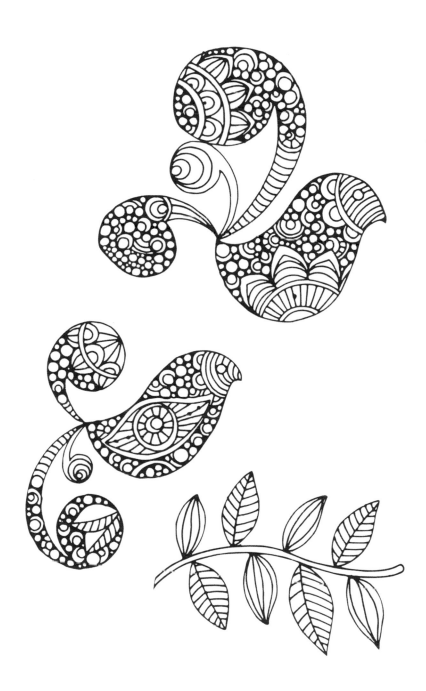

Make the most of yourself,
for that is all there is of you.

—Ralph Waldo Emerson

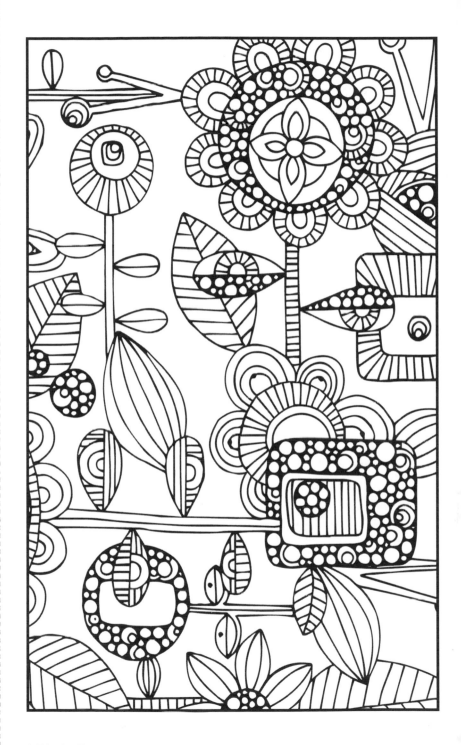

A friend is one who overlooks
your broken fence and admires
the flowers in your garden.

—Unknown

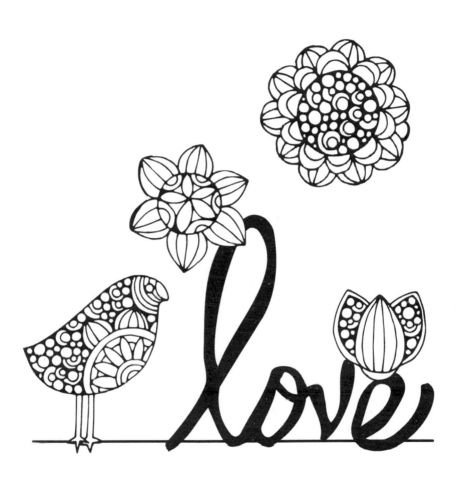

Love the life you live.
Live the life you love.

—**Bob Marley**

_____
_____
_____
_____
_____
_____
_____
_____
_____
_____
_____

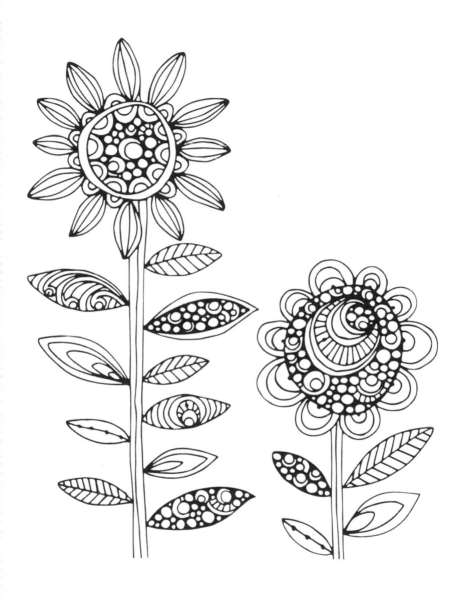

Bloom where you are planted.

—Unknown

_____
_____
_____
_____
_____
_____
_____
_____
_____
_____
_____